NFT SECRETS:

HOW PEOPLE ARE MAKING MASSIVE 100X GAINS
FROM NON FUNGIBLE TOKENS AND CRYPTO ART |
DISCOVER MY TOP PICKS FOR 2021 AND THE EASIEST
WAY TO TURN YOUR ART INTO AN NFT!

D1810220

Table of Contents

Introduction

What you will find in this book

This book will discuss everything about Non-fungible tokens (NFTs). The non-fungible token (NFT) garnered major mainstream media attention in 2020. It has been regarded as one of the most innovative blockchain technologies and has generated huge interest among developers, investors and customers alike.

NFTs are transforming the system of digital content ownership, thus giving content creators a whole new degree of control over their work, especially with regards to the worlds of digital art and collectibles. By the time you get to the end of this book you will have learned everything there is to know about NFTs – what they are, how they work, how to buy and sell them and the risks involved.

Why you should read this book

With buzzwords like NFT, cryptographic tokens and cryptoart the topic becomes confusing real quick, doesn't it? Are you amongst the people who are wondering what the heck everybody is talking about and whether you should consider buying or selling NFTs? Are you looking for someone to explain this craze in simple terms? If so this book is for you. This eye-opening guidebook will give you a brief basic knowledge of the history, principles, as well as pros and cons of cryptographic tokens and info on how to buy and sell NFTs. The goal is to give you answers to your most pressing questions, including whether NFTs are worthwhile considering as digital assets. Without further ado let's get started.

Chapter 1: Non Fungible Tokens

What Is Fungibility?

Fungible, in brief, means that a good or a commodity is easily interchangeable for any other, because each of its parts is indistinguishable from another part.

Many of the goods ideal for an exchange or trade process are fungible goods, such as money. It's irrelevant that you possess one specific, particular $100 bill in order for it to have that $100 dollar value. Any and every genuine bill that says $100 on it will have that value and is interchangeable with any other bill of that same value and can even be split up into five $20 bills that add up to that amount. Another example of a fungible good is gold, since one ounce of gold is equivalent to another ounce of gold, whether that's in the form of a coin or gold nugget.

Since fungible goods have no distinguishing characteristics from others of the same kind, they are often sold in bulk. Examples are grains or the same grade of oil. Another indicator that those goods or commodities may be fungible are when they are sold by weight or number. Bitcoin is also a fungible token. One bitcoin is one bitcoin.

Non-Fungibles

Assets like diamonds, land or owned cars are not fungible because each unit has unique one-of-a-kind qualities that add or subtract value. Two of 'the same' won't be equal and are not interchangeable.

To better understand what non-fungible tokens are, it is necessary to know the meaning of the two major terms: token, and non-fungible.

The word "token" in the phrase refers to a digital token which is a cryptographic certificate for an object or item. Tokens represent an asset or specific use and reside on their blockchain.

"Nonfungible has to do with a token having unique attributes and features which makes it difficult to exchange for another similar token. This means that the token cannot be directly exchanged for something else which has the same worth. For example, banknotes are fungible because they can be exchanged for other banknotes which possess the same value.

Nonfungible tokens (NFTs) are unique collectible digital assets which exist on a blockchain. NFTs are exceptional, so there's no characterized worth to any of them and they can't be traded. For instance, you have a FC Barcelona pullover endorsed by Lionel Messi. Of course, you could trade with somebody for another shirt of a similar club, yet the one you would get would definitely not be equivalent to the one you parted with.

To characterize the genuine significance of NFT, we need to comprehend the idea of "substitutability". The word may sound confounded, yet it is a straightforward thought, and we can relate it to every day life. Fundamentally, tradable things can be traded for another thing with a similar arrangement/portrayal in a 1:1 proportion. All consumables are essentially something very similar, so they can be traded. Money is an ideal illustration of fungible resources. Regardless of whether it is your US dollar note, 4the US dollar greenback found on the spot, or the US dollar note booted by the insane uncle, every one is valued at $1. Fungible merchandise/resources are fungible and are also very distinguishable. This implies that they can be added or part without changing the key idea of the venture. The U.S. dollar can generally be separated into any mix of coins that amount to 100 pennies and have a similar worth.

 Nonfungible tokens are also not divisible, just as you cannot give someone half of a movie ticket. Half a movie ticket would have no worth on its own and cannot be redeemed. Individuals can become very acquainted with the expression "blockchain," which is strongly a record of exchanges. For bitcoin and different sorts of virtual monetary standards, the blockchain keeps up record of token deals. This assists with holding of control inside the virtual monetary forms, because of the way that the log of exchanges affirms the measure of tokens being used, and likely gives proof of possession to exceptional proprietors. Because of the cryptographical idea of blockchains, any work to attempt to change one square will be spotted. This over the long haul keeps up blockchain security. In the event that the NFT is connected to the blockchain, all gatherings might have the option to check the legitimacy of the NFT. This is typically based on top of one of the current blockchains (like Ethereum). The possibility of NFT can be applied. For instance, when selling occasion tickets, NFT can be utilized for each pass to keep others from abusing it by keeping records on the blockchain.

Characteristics of Crypto Tokens

The main characteristic of NFTs or Non-Fungible Tokens is that they cannot be exchanged, as for example they can in the world of cryptocurrencies. Users or members cannot commercialize the NFTs without the consent of the creator. Nor can they be divided.

This "non-fungible" characteristic or that it cannot be divided, makes NFTs different from cryptocurrencies, which are identical to each other and that is why they are used as a "currency" or exchangeable or transferable asset.

To give us an idea, the NFTs propose the idea that the information that is transmitted with them, is inalienable or non-transferable, that is, if a work of art includes the data of a holder (buyer who acquires the work), This work will always include your identification data, during the time that the NFT will last (unlimitedly), so that security and transparency is maximum.

The disruptive use and popularity of NFT tokenization comes from the implementation in digital files, since as it is known, today most artistic works are created on digital and computer media, and most will not be physically transformed as it could be a sculpture or a painting by Picasso. For this reason, the use of NFTs is key to allow the collectible work, unique since its creation and not replicable (falsifiable), belongs, from start to finish, to the same person (or company).

This is the "magic" of Blockchain technology,

• This type of token is indivisible, that is, it cannot be divided into smaller or smaller denominations. They exist as a whole article.

• They are indestructible, since the data of these digital assets are stored in blocks through smart contracts and as a result of this, the tokens cannot be replicated, destroyed or eliminated.

• The ownership of NFTs is immutable, which means that collectors and gamers own them, not the big companies that create them.

● Another advantage of these tokens is that they are verifiable, as they can store historical property data within the blockchain. This allows the original creator to be traced and therefore allows the authentication of the pieces without having to resort to third parties to verify them.

Given the hype surrounding NFTs, it's worth asking whether there are any benefits of NFTs over other blockchain-based asset types.

Here are the top characteristics of NFTs:

1. Ownership

The ownership and non-fungibility of NFTs means that owners have full control over their assets and no one else can claim ownership over it. This provides a clear level of security for both developers and users when using NFTs in their applications and games.

For example, if you own a rare asset in a game or application, you know that it is safe and no one else can claim ownership over it. This means that there is no risk of losing your rare asset because it is non-fungible.

2. Transferability

In addition, NFTs are easier to transfer than many other blockchain-based assets because they can be represented by a unique ID number. This ID number can be used by the owner of an asset to quickly and easily trade or sell their asset without having to provide much additional information.

This makes it easy for people to trade or sell their assets, and makes it easier for users of applications and games that use NFTs. For example, a game developer might allow players to quickly sell or trade their rare items with other players using a blockchain-based auction system built into the game. This could be done with a simple transaction ID rather than providing much more information about the asset, like its location in the game or its level of rarity.

Another example is a digital art gallery that allows people to trade or sell their digital artworks quickly and easily. A blockchain-based system could be used to track the ownership of a digital artwork, and allow users to quickly trade or sell their assets using a simple ID number.

3. Authenticity

The authenticity of NFTs is also a key benefit. This is because the blockchain makes it easy to prove that an asset is authentic.

For example, if you are using a game or application that uses NFTs, you can be sure that the assets you have are genuine and not counterfeit. You can easily check this using a blockchain explorer like Etherscan.io or by checking a digital signature or fingerprint of the asset in the game or application.

4. Security

The security of NFTs is also one of their key benefits. Because they are represented by a unique ID number, there is no way for someone to "copy" or "clone" an NFT. This means that you can always be sure that your assets are secure and safe from being copied or stolen by someone else.

This is particularly important when using NFTs in applications and games where rare items are used as a form of reward or achievement system for players. For example, if you are using a game that uses NFTs as rewards for players who complete certain levels, you can be sure that those rewards aren't counterfeit because they can't be copied or faked in any way.

5. Customization

The customization of NFTs is also a key benefit. This is because NFTs can be easily customized by developers and users to represent anything they want.

For example, a game developer might create a new type of virtual sword in their game that can be used by players to attack enemies. They could then customize the sword using a set of features that represent the properties of the sword, like its size, length, weight, and number of attack points. This would make it possible for players to collect unique swords with different features and stats that would give them an advantage over other players in the game.

6. Permissionless

The permissionless nature of NFTs is also a key benefit. This is because NFTs can be used by anyone, without needing permission from anyone else.

This means that developers can quickly and easily create new assets and tokens for their applications and games without having to get approval from anyone else first. This provides a level of freedom for developers that isn't possible with other blockchain-based assets like tokens or coins. It also means that they don't have to worry about any restrictions on the types of assets they create or how many they make available in their applications or games.

7. Decentralization

This is a really cool topic. It's the idea that blockchains allow people to create their own assets. With this technology, you can create a token that represents a specific item or piece of property. It's essentially a digital asset that can be owned and transferred. This means that there is no need for a middleman like an auction house or real estate agent.

As NFTs rely on the blockchain, they are always decentralised. This means that you don't have to trust a third party to manage your assets. The blockchain is completely transparent and you can see everything that is happening with your digital asset. This means that there is no chance of the item being taken away from you or altered in any way.

8. Transparency

Transparency is an important part of the blockchain technology behind NFTs. Every transaction made on the blockchain is publicly available for everyone to see. This allows for complete transparency and there is no chance of anyone altering your data without being caught.

9. Easy Trading

NFTs allow for easy trading between users. They can be traded as many times as you want and are often easier to sell than physical items like paintings or cars. You simply create a digital token representing the item, then put it up for sale on an exchange where people can buy it using cryptocurrencies like Bitcoin or Ethereum (there are also exchanges for NFTs themselves). The token represents the item in question and if you decide to sell it, all that needs to happen is the token being transferred from one user to another. The item itself doesn't need to be transferred because it already exists on the blockchain.

Chapter 2: NFT

What are non-fungible tokens?

Nonfungible tokens (NFTs) are a piece of metadata that include the image, file or video of a piece of digital artwork, along with a unique identifier link that holds info on the creator of that file, a datastamp, associated smart contracts or text, and buyer information. This data is attached to a 'token' that gets stored in a blockchain.

You can think of an individual piece of cryptoart (NFT) as a trading card (like those Pokémon cards that have value as a collectible).

The value of this digital collectible is affected by the general trust in NFT as a concept, the trust in cryptocurrency (Ether) in general and the Ethereum blockchain network NFTs are traded on.

NFTs value is calculated in the cryptocurrency Ether (ETH) and is being sold and bought through the Ethereum blockchain network. 1 ETH was worth between approximately $1,400 USD and $2,000 USD in Feb/ early March of 2021, as a broad snapshot in time, keeping in mind that it's a highly volatile market.

To better understand what non-fungible tokens are, it is necessary to know the meaning of the two major terms: token, and non-fungible.

The word "token" in the phrase refers to a digital token which is a cryptographic certificate for an object or item. Tokens represent an asset or specific use and reside on their blockchain.

To characterize the genuine significance of NFT, we need to comprehend the idea of "substitutability". The word may sound confounded, yet it is a straightforward thought, and we can relate it to every day life. Fundamentally, tradable things can be traded for another thing with a similar arrangement/portrayal in a 1:1 proportion. All consumables are essentially something very similar, so they can be traded. Money is an ideal illustration of fungible resources. Regardless of whether it is your US dollar note, 4the US dollar greenback found on the spot, or the US dollar note booted by the insane uncle, every one is valued at $1. Fungible merchandise/resources are fungible and are also very distinguishable. This implies that they can be added or part without changing the key idea of the venture. The U.S. dollar can generally be separated into any mix of coins that amount to 100 pennies and have a similar worth.

Nonfungible tokens are also not divisible, just as you cannot give someone half of a movie ticket. Half a movie ticket would have no worth on its own and cannot be redeemed. Individuals can become very acquainted with the expression "blockchain," which is strongly a record of exchanges. For bitcoin and different sorts of virtual monetary standards, the blockchain keeps up record of token deals. This assists with holding of control inside the virtual monetary forms, because of the way that the log of exchanges affirms the measure of tokens being used, and likely gives proof of possession to exceptional proprietors. Because of the cryptographical idea of blockchains, any work to attempt to change one square will be spotted. This over the long haul keeps up blockchain security. In the event that the NFT is connected to the blockchain, all gatherings might have the option to check the legitimacy of the NFT. This is typically based on top of one of the current blockchains (like Ethereum). The possibility of NFT can be applied. For instance, when selling occasion tickets, NFT can be utilized for each pass to keep others from abusing it by keeping records on the blockchain.

Examples of non-fungible tokens

Athletic apparel organization Nike created a NFT project in December 2019, a framework considered CryptoKicks that it would use to give NFTs for footwear. CryptoKick tokens would be utilized to connect actual shoes with computerized renditions with a scope of utilizations, including confirming their credibility, exchanging them on advanced commercial centers, utilizing them in video gaming and other virtual conditions, and advising clients when virtual shoe plans are produced. The computerized shoes could change in appearance and worth dependent on changes to the actual shoes, like age and use, which would influence their worth.

In February 2021, Crossroads, an activity by advanced craftsman Mike Winkelmann, who is known as Beeple, was exchanged for $6.6m on a NFT stage called Nifty Gateway. That far outperformed the past record for a solitary NFT of $1.55m and was multiple times the $66,666.60 the work initially sold for in November 2020.

In August 2020, the Museum of Crypto Art (MOCA) left an indelible mark on the world for what was at the time the greatest purchase on NFT craftsmanship business platform Nifty Gateway, obtaining "Picasso's Bull" by expert Trevor Jones for $55,555.55 worth of Ether — an arrangement that Nifty Gateway portrayed as a critical accomplishment in the workmanship world that affirmed NFTs as another instrument of craftsmanship. MOCA set #20 in the Cointelegraph's best 100 most noticeable people in Blockchain 2020.

In February 2021, the craftsman Grimes sold about $6 million worth of tokens tending to cutting edge craftsmanship on Nifty Gateway. Later in February of 2021, a NFT tending to the picture energy Nyan Cat was sold in a web business community for barely short of US$600,000.

In March 2021, sales management firm Christie's sold a ton from craftsman Mike Winkelmann, known as "Beeple," for $69.3 million. As Christie's is a significant barker that manages exceptionally important workmanship, this isn't strange until you understand that the deal wasn't for a customary fine art. The offer of "Everyday - The First 5,000 Days" is professed to be the first for a simply advanced masterpiece through a significant sales management firm. A composition of Beeple's day by day advanced craftsmanship creation, the work shows the craftsman's movement over numerous years, remembering changes for procedure and style. The closeout victor was recognized as "Metakovan," the unknown boss agent of the NFT-driven asset Metapurse. For their $69 million, the triumphant bidder obtained the non-fungible token (NFT) connected to the fine art. Beeple's craft additionally procured the differentiation of being the costliest NFT at any point sold, just as the third-most-costly work of art sold at closeout by a living craftsman.

History of nonfungible tokens

The basic idea of non-fungible tokens originated in 2012 through what was then called Colored Coins. Colored Coins can be as small as a satoshi, the smallest unit of a Bitcoin. Just like with NFT's they were used to represent various types of assets in the form of coupons, subscriptions, access tokens or digital collectibles, to name a few. Without going into detail, the system was flawed. Yet, many people realized that there's a huge potential for issuing assets onto blockchains. So in 2014 the financial platform Counterparty was founded. Projects and assets included a trading card game and meme trading. Via Counterparty, the game creators of Spells of Genesis provided in-game assets and were amongst the first ones to launch Initial Coin Offerings (ICOs), which is the cryptocurrency industry's equivalent to an initial public offering (IPO), with a similar concept to crowdfunding.

In 2016, Force of Will, another popular trading card game, also used Counterparty's platform. It became the 4th ranked card game by sales in North America. Rare Peeps meme followed in the same year.

As Ethereum became more popular in 2017, memes started to be traded there as well. Peperium also used Ethereum as their decentralized meme marketplace and trading card game platform. Next were CryptoPunks, 10,000 unique punk characters. They were probably the ones who paved the way for Cryptoart, along with CryptoKitties.

What can NFTs be used for?

Uses of NFTs in Accounting

Accounting is concerned with financial management and accountability. A nonfungible token is a digital asset which can serve various purposes and in this chapter, we examine the relationship between the uses of nonfungible tokens and the field of accounting. The ways a nonfungible token can be useful in accounting are examined below:

1. Identity management

Identity management is very pertinent in today's world which is interconnected than ever. Identity management is useful in accounting because it helps financial workers track fraudulent activities easily. Accountants can easily trace the identity of transactions involving a nonfungible token because of the ERC721 standard.

Identity management can also help curb crime by speeding up the investigation process and the identification of criminals involved in a crime. It can also enable people prove their identity in the absence of physical documents or evidence.

It is easier to move from one place to another because of modern means of transportation which are faster as well.

2. Collateral for loan

There are many fintech companies that offer loans to people who need money urgently. There are criteria an individual who seeks a loan must meet before the loan can be granted to him. One of the requirements that makes a person eligible to access a loan is the ability to repay the loan when due and the possession of a collateral which may he converted by the company if the borrower defaults.

A nonfungible is readily available and can become useful collateral when needed. Apart from fintech companies, many local lenders accept nonfungible tokens as collateral because of their unique nature, portability and flexibility. A valuable nonfungible token can serve as good collateral.

3. Used to allocate indivisible property

A Nonfungible token makes it easier to allocate properties that cannot be divisible or are hard to divide. This means those who have a share in the property can own different fractions of the digital copy of the property which could not have been possible with a physical property.

For example, if an artist and a painter owned a physical piece of art and the painter wants to sell it off, it would be difficult for the painter to sell it out if the artist disagrees. If the art work exists digitally as a nonfungible token, the painter can easily sell his fraction to a buyer who will now be the owner of his fraction of the digital art work (nonfungible token) while the artist still retains his fraction of the artwork like he wished. This means that the art work would now belong to the artist and the buyer who bought the painter's part. It would be difficult to achieve such process with a physical artwork.

4. Simplifies real estate trading

With nonfungible tokens, a real estate trader does not need to travel long distances before he can trade his real estate. A digital representation of the real estate property will be easier to trade. This is another advantage a nonfungible token has over a physical property.

The existence of a unique code or data on every nonfungible token helps to prevent fraud. It ensures that only one person can claim the ownership of a certain property at any point in time. Even if the property is jointly owned, it still remains one unique property. This prevents buyers from suffering fraud or misrepresentation that may occur if an imitation of a nonfungible token is sold. The idea of a nonfungible token eliminates most practices of misrepresentation and elements of fraud that occur in real estate transactions.

5. Event tickets

The technology of nonfungible tokens is very useful in the administration of event tickets. To attend an event like a wedding ceremony, you need to be invited. If you want to attend an event where your favorite celebrity performs, you will most likely pay for the ticket of the event. There are many protocols that must be observed for an event to be successful.

Advanced Art.

Advanced workmanship was part of the early use cases of non-fungible tokens, in cognizance of the capacity of blockchain innovation to guarantee the remarkable mark and responsibility for.

Games.

NFTs can likewise be utilized to address in-game resources which are constrained by the client instead of the game engineer. The main utilization of non-fungible tokens in gaming was executed by Tokenzone utilizing a brought together methodology. NFTs permit resources for be exchanged on outsider commercial centers without authorization from the game engineer. Computerized Assets At the point when we refer to Decentraland, individuals can purchase virtual land. Another model more recognizable to home is the ENS (Ether Name Service), and it utilizes NFT's for its. Ether spaces to assist with purchasing and trading.

Nonfungible tokens are critical for vetting for ID misrepresentation. Cases of things which may be made digital to address personality incorporate capabilities, clinical reports, and looks. Besides, computerized makers can transform their items into NFTs for patent rights thoughts. NFT's utilization to check character includes transforming actual sports tickets into *nonfungible tokens to* stay away from fakes.

NFT use cases

Decentralized applications (Dapps) on the blockchain use NFTs for investment purposes, digital identities, virtual assets, fine art, trading cards **etc.** Since the explosion of NFTs in the cryptospace in 2017 coincidentally aided by the ICO boom, there has been significant growth in the crypto-collectible market with over a hundred successful NFT projects. Here are a few popular ones:

Cryptopunks – a huge success, Cryptopunks will be recorded in history forever (and also in the blockchain). Created in 2017 by

Larva Labs, the project initially created 10 000 unique characters distributed for free. Currently, they can be sold and purchased in marketplaces like OpenSea or on the Larva Labs website. The most expensive CryptoPunks are currently traded for a few million dollars. This one is **my favourite punk**. Should I buy one?

CryptoKitties – another big hit. Some of the kitties are being traded for close to one million dollars. Created in 2007, the Cryptokitties can breed to create new kitties with new "catributes". Each kittie is unique and cannot be replicated.

Sorare – a global fantasy football game using licensed football cards. Each player represents a card backed by an ERC-721 token. Each player card is unique and is owned by the gamer. The cards are validated in the Ethereum blockchain, and their value can appreciate or depreciate based on the market.

ENS Domains – Ethereum Naming Service allows creating .eth domains that can be used for different purposes, including to receive crypto. The ENS domains are immutable and censorship-resistant because they are distributed in the blockchain. **Unstoppabledomains** is another service similar to ENS domains.

Gods Unchained – another cool card game that allows users to own unique cards represented by ERC-721 tokens.

Decentraland - a virtual reality platform that is wholly owned by users, powered by the Ethereum blockchain. Users can create, experience, and monetize content and applications.

Binance Collectibles - created in 2018 as a series of holiday-themed NFTs to serve as prizes for a festive engagement campaign during the season of giving. The ERC-1155, which allows both fungible and nonfungible tokens under the same contract, was used.

MyCryptons - digital collectibles of public figures, ranging from Head of States to celebrities like Oprah Winfrey, can be collected and sold.

SuperRare - a blockchain project that is creating NFT that enables digital artists to link an image or a GIF they've created to a token.

Nifty Gateway - a marketplace to buy and sell NFTs that represent artwork or limited edition items created by artists, brands and content creators. Another great platform for artists to use.

Legends of Crypto – LoC is an NFT game that allows users to collect rare NFT cards with characters from the crypto universe. Users can also play the Legends of Crypto game and win new NFT cards.

How are NFTs stored?

ERC-721 smart contracts are stored on the Ethereum blockchain, and as a result, NFTs can be stored in any Ethereum wallet that supports ERC-721 tokens. Some of the most popular wallets for storing ERC-721 tokens include:

MetaMask: This browser extension is available for both Chrome and Firefox. It can be used to interact with websites that support Ethereum by creating and signing transactions on the blockchain. It also allows users to access their Ethereum wallet, which can be used to store ERC-721 tokens. MetaMask currently has more than 500,000 active users worldwide.

Coinbase Wallet: This wallet is available on both iOS and Android platforms, and it can be used to store any cryptocurrency that is supported by Coinbase, including Ether (ETH), Bitcoin (BTC), Litecoin (LTC), and more than 90 other coins and tokens. It also supports Ethereum's ERC-20 standard, which means it can be used to store ERC-20 tokens like CryptoKitties' own proprietary KittyWallet app. As of January 2019, Coinbase Wallet has been downloaded more than 100,000 times.

MyEtherWallet: This is a popular open-source wallet that can be used to store ERC-20 tokens, as well as other types of tokens that are supported by Ethereum. It can be used to store any ERC-20 token that is created using the Ethereum blockchain.

MyCrypto: This is another open-source wallet that can be used to store Ether (ETH), ERC-20 tokens, and other types of tokens that are supported by Ethereum. It is also compatible with ERC-721 smart contracts, which means it can be used to store NFTs.

MetaMask, Coinbase Wallet, MyEtherWallet, and MyCrypto are all compatible with CryptoKitties' KittyWallet app. They are also compatible with any other ERC-721 smart contract or application that supports NFTs and can issue new NFTs at any time to its owner or owners. CryptoKitties itself was the first ever blockchain game to launch an NFT marketplace for users to buy, sell, and breed their digital cats; it has since been followed by several other blockchain games such as CryptoAlpaca, CryptoFighters, and EtherTanks.

Advantages of NFTs

They make it possible to evaluate and protect sources of investment in high-quality products.

They allow the source and security to be traced on the blockchain and verified through secure storage in the customs warehouse.

Token holders can obtain asset financing based on the value of the product.

In this way, NFT technology allows producers or creators to carry out investment transactions in products, for example, in bottled and boxed wine, which can vary their value in the market.

Protect the quality and value of products with NFT technology

The quality and value of the products will be protected with the metadata and information in the NFT Tokens, which will be constantly verified by the blockchain.

In sectors where counterfeiting abounds and the origin of the products is doubted, whether in the textile industry or that of alcoholic beverages, for example wines, the stamping of time, place, state of preservation of the product, origin of the raw material and all other data related to the value of the product in the market and its authenticity, will be protected and guaranteed in the product information.

Non-fungible NFT tokens combat product and brand counterfeits

If the physical product industries take on this technology as a guarantee of authenticity and registration of information, intellectual and industrial property will increase in value exponentially.

The NFT tokens used in these types of products include a non-fungible or manipulable ERC-721 token structure. As is typical of NFT technology, it is implemented on the Ethereum blockchain. Smart contracts track the ownership, provenance, and transaction history of tokens and serve as a confirmation standard for authenticity and invariance that all other tokens validate and confirm. With the use of NFT tokens, each product is assigned a token with a unique identifier and its attributes are stored as detailed metadata.

On a blockchain, NFTs reflecting physical or digital artwork, eliminates the need for middlemen, thereby enabling artists to interact directly with their audiences. They can also help businesses develop their processes.

Non-fungible tokens are also great for managing identities. Consider physical passports, which must be shown at any point of entry and exit.

It is possible to simplify the entry and exit processes for different jurisdictions by transforming individual passports into NFTs, each with its unique characteristics for identification. Furthermore, NFTs may also be used for managing identities in the digital world.

By dividing tangible assets such as real estate, investing can also be democratized by NFTs. A digital real estate asset is much easier to be shared among different owners than a physical one. This tokenization function does not have to be limited to real estate; it can be applied to other assets like artworks.

The most promising NFT possibility lies in the development of new markets and investment types. Consider a real estate piece parceled out into several sections, each of which includes various characteristics and property styles. One division might be situated near a beach, while another is an entertainment center, and another, a residential area.

Based on its features, a piece of land is special, priced differently, and represented by an NFT. By integrating the relevant metadata into each specific NFT, real estate trading, which is a complicated and bureaucratic operation, can be streamlined.

Decentraland, an Ethereum-based virtual reality network, has already executed such a design. As NFTs become more advanced and incorporated into financial infrastructure, the idea of tokenized pieces of land with varying values and locations might be able to be implemented in the physical world.

1. **Limited:** NFTs have a limited supply, which adds to their appeal. NFT creators can generate an infinite number of non-

fungible tokens, and they often alter the tokens to maximize interest.

2. *Indivisible:* NFTs are indivisible into smaller units in the vast majority of cases. If you either pay the full price of a digital item, or you don't buy at all.

3. *Unique:* NFTs have a good information tab that illustrates what makes them special. This information is completely safe and accurate.

4. *Easy to Transfer:* NFTs are easily transferable because they are bought and sold on specialized marketplaces. The use of NFTs is contingent on their uniqueness.

5. *Keeping Rights to Ownership*: This refers to a decentralized platform worth of NFTs in which the data cannot be altered by any future buyer.

Why Is NFT Not Called A Digital Coin?

Although people sometimes refer to the same digital asset when they use the term 'coin' or 'token', there's actually a big difference between crypto coins and crypto tokens.

Digital (Crypto) Coin

You may be familiar with the term Bitcoin, which is an asset (in form of data, not as an actual coin) that it's native to its own blockchain, called Bitcoin blockchain in this case. Ether, as another example of a crypto currency coin operates and functions on the Ethereum blockchain.

Think of digital coins such as Bitcoin, Litecoin and Monero as cash in your wallet. What you can do with digital coins is either pay for goods and services, store them (just like the coins you'd keep in your piggy bank, if that's still a thing) or you use them as a unit of account, meaning, the things that you buy can be priced in Bitcoin, too.

Some digital coins, and Ether is one example of that, can do more than just being useful as a form of money.

Digital (Crypto) Token

Digital tokens can represent a physical thing, for example. Since you can't physically put your house into the smart contract, you can use a token that represents your house.

Another example would be smart contracts that allow users to buy and sell electricity on the blockchain. The tokens then represent a certain amount of energy.

Token can be created and built on existing blockchains. Ethereum is the most popular network platform. Anyone / company can make their own custom token Ethereum can then create and facilitate smart contracts. Digital coins (Ether) are needed to fund the mining costs and to send tokens. Meaning, Ether is the form of money that pays the computers which verify the transactions on the Ethereum network.

Pros And Cons Of NFTS

Now that you've gained some basic insights and principles of how the system works, let's talk about pros and cons of NFTs, or what is being hyped and perceived as being pros and cons. Again, please use first principle thinking and make up your own mind, questioning assumptions and statements made by others than yourself.

Pros

From an artist's perspective, the pros include that NFTs allow artists to monetize digital artwork without a middleman like a gallery. The marketplaces listed above can however be seen as a middleman. The advantage of using them, rather than minting your own NFTs on the open Ethereum blockchain directly, is that most platforms allow you to report fakes and counterfeits. Most platforms also have tools to boost the artists' visibility and have a reach that is hard to match if you go solo. It's in the marketplaces best interest to come across as supportive, as their business model depends on it. Therefore your art's value may increase for the simply fact that you're using a reputable marketplace.

Middlemen such as auction houses could use private blockchains to track provenance, they wouldn't have to worry about keeping paper records or detecting art forgery and could unify digital artwork in a single digital system. It would be an add-on to their existing way of selling physical art.

From a buyer's perspective, NFTs may get perceived like investing in the stock market, hoping that it's an ongoing upward trend and 'the next big thing to get into' to grow your wealth.

Letting you be your own judge, Cryptoart.io/artists is a website that gives you a good overview of artists, number of artworks sold and selling price, and is also comparing different marketplaces.

Of course, this a one-sided view and other perspectives should be taken into consideration, one of them being the environmental aspect.

Cons

The value of digital collectibles is affected by the general trust in NFT as a concept, the trust in cryptocurrency (Ether) in general and the Ethereum blockchain network NFTs are traded on. And unethical players may be able to manipulate price and demand.

Currently there's no regulatory intellectual property protection structure in place to prevent copyrighted works of art from being minted into and sold as NFTs. Once an FTS is minted, there is no way to remove it from the blockchain.

Regarding smart contracts: Certain contents such as the idea of including royalties for the artist on a resale depend entirely on the goodwill of the party, as there's no official legal protection in this regard.

One thing I'd like to talk about in more detail are the ecological costs from the huge amount of data, gas and energy that's needed, in order to run blockchain and do the mining of the tokens.

What is meant by ecological costs?

Energy Costs

This energy consumption refers to the electricity that miners use in the Proof of Work process, in order to validate transactions and earn Ether (ETH) as a reward.

For context: Minting artwork on the blockchain can use somewhere between weeks, months or even years of an average EU or US citizen's energy consumption. You can track the ecological cost of NFTs on Cryptoart.wtf or digiconomist.net/Ethereum-energy/consumption.

CO_2

Marketplace Superrare is saying that Ethereum's carbon emissions are tied to price, not volume. In their article ***No, CryptoArtists Aren't Harming the Planet*** they were comparing the Ethereum network to a train, using it as a metaphor to argue that 'the train will run whether or not the seats (NFTs) are filled.' They were saying if no one would be using the Ethereum app and no transaction were sent, the carbon emission of the network would stay unchanged.

One factor that's not mentioned in the article is that seats on trains become more expensive when trains are full. In that case the whole blockchain network emits more CO_2.

Transaction Fees Paid in Gas

There's a fee for transactions sent to the network to avoid spam, and it's paid in gas. Gas transactions cost the sender more money, but apparently don't correlate with higher carbon emissions, Superrare is saying in that same article I mentioned above. (Keep in mind, Superrare is a NFT marketplace.)

Proof of Work

Proof of Work is a necessary step in the process of validating blocks on the blockchain. Wiki is defining it as one party (the prover) proves to others (the verifiers) that a certain amount of computational effort has been expended for some purpose.

The more complex the blocks get, the more a computer needs to work and the more energy will get used.

A study in 2020 from the University of New Mexico concluded that in 2018, each $1 of Bitcoin value created was responsible for $0.49 in health and climate damages in the US and $0.37 in China.

Ethereum is apparently using less energy than Bitcoin.

The Ethereum network's annual energy consumption is hovering around 25.37 TWh, which is roughly the annual energy consumption of Ecuador.

That may be hard to grasp, so let me give you a more visual example. One single Ethereum transaction carbon footprint is the equivalent of watching YouTube for – take a guess! 4,397 hours! Assuming the very high number of watching four hours of YouTube every day, that would add up to over 1,000 days, which is just about three full years.

Non-fungible token myths

Several myths are surrounding NFTs and non-fungible tokens. This is understandable, considering that most of these myths have been around for years. Here's a list of some of the more common myths.

1) *Myth*: "Ethereum has thousands of pending transactions" – This is one of the most common misconceptions about Ethereum. It reveals a misunderstanding about how blockchains work and how they process data. In fact, the amount of pending transactions has nothing to do with the number of people using the network or its popularity. It simply means that there are a lot of pending transactions in this block. This is actually a good thing because it means that many developers and users are using Ethereum. The more people who use Ethereum, the more valuable it becomes.

2) *Myth*: "NFTs are a scam" – This is another common misconception about NFTs. This is true in some markets, but it is not the case in most cases. A few years ago, this was true because people were unfamiliar with the concept of non-fungible tokens. However, as time went on and more people understood what they were, this myth died out. Today, many professional traders who understand the benefits of NFTs and blockchain technology are starting to view them as an investment rather than a scam.

This was shown by the fact that nine percent of all NFTs were traded on the Ethereum network during 2018.

3) *Myth*: "NFTs are too volatile" – This is another common misconception about non-fungible tokens. The price of an NFT will go up and down, just like any other coin or token. This is because it is not linked to a specific item and can be used in any number of games. That is why it can be traded for items in games as well as real-world assets.

4) Myth: "NFTs are too expensive" – This is not true at all. The price of NFTs varies, but the average cost is equivalent to that of other cryptocurrencies, which are already cheap compared to traditional currencies. This means you can get as many NFTs as you want for a fraction of the cost of a traditional currency.

5) Myth: "NFTs are too complicated and hard to create" – This is not true, either. It all depends on the game developer and which blockchain platform they are using. Since there are so many different types of blockchain platforms, developers will be able to use whichever one they prefer. However, if they are using Ethereum, they can use NFT-Crowdfund to create their own NFT token. This means they can rely on a protocol to create their own NFT without having to learn a new programming language or build their own smart contracts. The only thing they will need is some knowledge about Ethereum and how it works.

6) Myth: "NFTs don't bring value to the gaming industry" – This is another common misconception about non-fungible tokens. There are a lot of games that allow you to collect NFTs. This means that these features can increase the value of an NFT. After all, NFTs can be used in many different forms, including virtual items in games such as CryptoKitties and Spells of Genesis.

Chapter 3: How they works

How do NFTs work?

NFTs are very important to Ethereum blockchain so they are singular tokens with additional data put away in them. That additional data is the significant part, which permits them to appear as craftsmanship, music, video, (etc), as JPGS, MP3s, recordings, GIFs and that's just the beginning. Since they hold esteem, *they can be purchased* and sold actually like different kinds of craftsmanship – and, as with actual workmanship, the worth is generally set by the market and by request. This shouldn't imply that there's just a single advanced rendition of a NFT craftsmanship accessible on the commercial center, however. Similarly, as craftsmanship prints *of a unique* are made, utilized, purchased and sold, duplicates of a NFT are as yet legitimate *pieces of the blockchain* – yet they won't hold a similar worth as the former. What's more, don't go reasoning you've hacked the situation by right-clicking and saving the picture of a NFT, by the same token. That will not make you a tycoon on the grounds that your downloaded document will not hold the data that makes it part of the Ethereum blockchain.

NFTs contrast from cryptographic forms of money *like Bitcoin (BTC), Ether (ETH) or* Cardano (ADA) that go about as advanced coins. NFTs are tokens that address advanced or actual resources *– for instance, a piece of* craftsmanship, music, or even conceivably land – and contain extra data that a coin would not convey. *NFTs can be* utilized to verify masterpieces and different collectibles.

What is therefore the significance? A *token is a* unit of cash. *A non-fungible token* is one that can't be traded for something different. For instance, a banknote is fungible in that it very well may be traded for different banknotes conveying a similar worth, anyway a boarding pass is non-fungible as it conveys novel data and can't be utilized instead of another traveler's ticket. Similarly, a *NFT is a* remarkable symbolic *that can be* utilized to appropriate and check possession *through the blockchain.* Nonfungible tokens can likewise be made on other brilliant agreement empowered blockchains with non-fungible symbolic instruments and backing. Despite *the fact that* Ethereum *was the first to* be broadly utilized, NEO, EOS and TRON currently have NFT principles. Nonfungible tokens and their keen agreements take into consideration point by point credits to be added, similar

44

to the personality of the proprietor, rich metadata, or secure document joins.

The intense **of non-fungible tokens** to permanently demonstrate computerized proprietorship is a significant movement for an inexorably advanced world. They could see blockchain's guarantee of trustless security utilized to proprietorship or trade of practically any resource. Similar to the test of blockchain to date, non-fungible tokens, their conventions and savvy contract innovation is as yet being created. Making decentralized applications and stages for the administration and production **of non-fungible tokens is** still generally convoluted. There is additionally the test of making a norm. Blockchain advancement is divided, numerous designers are dealing with their own undertakings. To be effective there may should be brought together conventions and interoperability.

As is the challenge of blockchain to date, non-fungible tokens, their protocols and smart contract technology is still being developed. Creating decentralized applications and platforms for the management and creation of non-fungible tokens is still relatively complicated. There is also the challenge of creating a standard. Blockchain development is fragmented, many developers are working on their own projects. To be successful there may need to be unified protocols and interoperability.

Tokens for the governance of the platform, when introduced, are one of the characteristics that will help the NFT projects to have more relevance. This feature was what helped DeFi at its early stages.

Non-fungible tokens are digital objects that can't be replicated or broken down into smaller chunks. On the surface, they function similarly to other crypto assets in that they are transferable, valuable, and based on blockchain technology.

NFTs, however, cannot be fractionalized like bitcoin, which can be divided into smaller units known as satoshi.

Decentraland and CryptoKitties, for example, based their NFTs on the Ethereum standard called ERC-721.

Other smart contract-enabled blockchains, like Binance Smart Chain (BSC), TRON, EOS, and NEO, have their own NFT specifications that allow NFT creations on their respective blockchains. ERC-1155, a new improved standard, was recently issued, enabling a single contract to have the fungible and non-fungible tokens together.

How are Nonfungible Tokens Created

The method of developing a NFT is known as "minting" – a reference to the manner in which an actual coin is stamped by a developer. NFTs are stamped through a NFT commercial center, where a developer transfers a computerized record and appoints attributes, for example, regardless of whether it is coincidental, has numerous duplicates or is extremely crucial to an assortment. When the NFT is made, the proprietor can sell it on the commercial center in a sale.

NFTs are developed by transferring a document, like a craftsmanship, to a NFT open trade market, like OpenSea, Known Origin or Rarible. This makes a duplicate of the document saved on the advanced record as a non-fungible token and it can be bought with cryptographic money and therefore exchangeable. Albeit a craftsman can sell a NFT addressing *a work, the* craftsman can still in any case lay claim to the patent rights *of the work and* make more *NFTs of* a resembling work. The purchaser *of the NFT* doesn't acquire restrictive admittance *to the work,* nor does the purchaser acquire ownership rights of the "first" advanced record. An individual who transfers a particular piece of work doesn't need to demonstrate that they are the first craftsman, and there have been various situations where workmanship was utilized for NFTs without the maker's consent.

NFTs can be created using a special smart contract called an "ERC-721 smart contract". ERC-721 smart contracts are designed to be used with Ethereum, and they can only be accessed by their owner or owners. They are similar to normal Ethereum smart contracts in that they have a unique address and can only be accessed by their owner or owners; however, they are different from normal Ethereum smart contracts in that they do not have any gas limit or gas price associated with them. In addition, the information stored on an ERC-721 smart contract cannot be changed once it is stored on the blockchain; any changes made to it will result in its permanent destruction. As a result, ERC-721 smart contracts cannot be used for transactions or data storage; they can only be used for creating NFTs.

Once an ERC-721 smart contract has been created, it can then issue new tokens at any time to its owner or owners. This process is known as "minting" on Ethereum; tokens are minted when new assets are added to the blockchain by creating a new smart contract.

Step by step minting NFTs

Disclosure: the NFT market is new at it's evolving at a very fast pace. I cannot guarantee that by the time you read this, the steps to create an NFT will be the same, nor can I guarantee that this content will be updated.

Step 0 – Ownership of the asset

Before creating an NFT, you need to make sure that you are either the creator or the owner of the asset/art piece you will tokenize. You must have a way to prove that you are the owner or creator.

Step 1 – Prepare the assets

Make sure that you have the file for the image. You can simply tokenize a JPEG/PNG, but it's better to also have the source file or a good quality file. If you are dealing with digital art, the TIFF, AI/EPS can also be shared in the sale process.

Step 2 – Select the marketplace and authenticate

Now we need to mint the NFT token. The token can be minted directly on OpenSea marketplace when you want to sell it, or you can mint it first on Rarible because on Rarible you can mint a token without actually having to sell it. Up to you to decide.

In this step by step, I assume that you already have your Metamask browser plugin installed and have an Ethereum wallet with some Ether.

On OpenSea, click create and connect your Metamask wallet (check wallets section). Login to your Metamask wallet by clicking the Metamask icon and click connect. Later you will also need Ether to pay the transaction fee to the network during the minting process, but for now, you don't need to spend money.

Once your wallet is connected, you are authenticated and identified on the website with your public key. It's similar to when you login using your Google or Facebook identity (also known as SAML/SSO – Single Sign-On).

Step 3 – Start to create the NFT by uploading a file

To create a new item, go ahead and click create. You will have to create a collection, and your NFTs can be part of a collection. You can make more collections in the future – for example, the 2D collection, 3D collection, **etc.**

Once you have created a collection, you are able to "add new item" to the collection. Click "add new item". You will be able to upload a file, and you will find a number of formats available: PNG, GIF, WEBP, MP4, MP3 and much more. You can select and upload your file here.

Step 4 – Create an IPFS link

It's important to highlight that the image itself it's not stored on the blockchain. What is stored on the blockchain is only metadata about the image, **i.e.** the hash of the file, name, timestamp and a link to the place where the file is stored. Blockchains are not good to store big files, and the files will always need to be stored somewhere else. In the case of OpenSea, they will take care of storing the image.

If you want the buyer to receive the high-resolution file or source file, you can also store this file in a storage service (IPFS, Google Drive, S3 or Dropbox) and share the link to the file in the field "Unlockable content". This file will be shared with the buyer once the purchase is completed.

To keep things more decentralized and keep the blockchain spirit here, instead of using a centralized storage service like Google Drive or Dropbox, let's use IPFS – Interplanetary File System. IPFS is not a blockchain, but it's a distributed peer-to-peer file system (similar to BitTorrent) that will allow us to store and share files.

The easiest way to use UPFS is Pinata. Go to Pinata.cloud and sign up if you didn't sign up yet. Once you have a Pinata account, go to your dashboard, and click upload. Select the file and upload it.

Once the file is uploaded, you will find a CID hash (content identifier), something like Qma4Jse7V6tZ7k3756iPv39tsMG6DhxUQrc42cKoAVVsbR.

This is the hash the will be linked to the image. Copy also the link for the image, go back to the OpenSea website, and paste it in the "Unlockable content" field. The link should look something like this:

https://gateway.pinata.cloud/ipfs/Qma4Jse7V6tZ7k375 6iPv39tsMG6DhxUQrc42cKoAVVsbR

Step 5 – NFT properties

Complete the additional properties and tags.

Finally, click create.

You will now have created the asset on the OpenSea website but it's still not listed for sale.

Step – 6 Sell the NFT

Go to your item page and click "Sell".

You can also set a "Set price". This is similar to Ebay's "Buy it now", and it's the price that you are willing to receive to sell your item immediately. The price can be listed in different cryptocurrencies, but the most common one is Ether (ETH, Ethereum's native currency).

You can also select "Highest bid". This is the auction option, and in this option, you can select the minimum bid, reserve price and auction expiration date.

Finally, click "Post your Listing".

Once you click, follow the steps to mint the token. Your Metamask window will prompt (if not, you need to click the

Metamask icon) and click sign. OpenSea doesn't charge any fees, but whenever you mint a new NFT, you will be writing data to the blockchain, and you will incur gas fees (i.e. fees to the Ethereum network).

Once you click "approve" it will prompt your Metamask wallet so that you pay for the fees. On your Metamask wallet, you can click "edit" to edit the fees and select slow or fast. Slow means that you will pay fewer gas fees, but the transaction can take longer to be settled in the blockchain (usually less than 1 hour).

The cost to mint a new NFT may be sometimes high considering that the Ethereum may be congested, but it will probably tend to be lower in the future.

Your NFT is now listed, and people will be able to bid for it or buy it.

How the process works

Easiest way to think of the process is the abbreviation C.M.E, which means Create-Mint-Earn. We will go over each part so that you have an understanding of each part of the process.

CREATE

As a digital artist you do what you love which is create your art! You will be able to create 3D, 2D, portrait, gifs, short motions, different arts you naturally believe in, using any of the tools you use on a day to day basis (illustrator, photoshop, Blender, etc).

The only requirement is that your dimensions are appropriate for the website platform to place it into

MINT

You will mint your art, which means validating(_stamping_) your artwork into the blockchain. This process helps you create a smart contract which holds information about your art and who it originally belongs to.

This is where ownership comes into play. If it is ever lost you can always find it using phrases if need be from your extension. There are fees you have to pay for each Artwork you mint.

In the crypto space it is called gas(Gwei) fee.

EARN

After you have minted your art you can place a set price or place a bid. Once your artwork is sold you receive cryptocurrency that can later be converted into USD. Wait there is MORE! Your artwork is yours so if your art is resold at a different price you as the artist receives royalties (*percentage of that profit*).

What Does Blockchain have To Do With Nfts, Cryptoart And Collectibles?

A blockchain is basically the database that stores all the data in blocks and keeps track of all the crypto currency transactions. Each block has a certain storage capacity for data. Once the storage of a block is full, a new block will get chained onto the previously filled block, forming a chain of data, as more blocks are added. Hence, the term 'blockchain'. All blockchains are databases.

By using the block system that gets chained together one after the other, it creates an irreversible timeline of data. Bitcoin consists of thousands of computers holding its blockchain, all operated by separate individuals or groups of people in different geographic locations. These computers that form Bitcoin's network are called nodes.

This guarantees that no single node within the network can alter data held within it. Because of this, the whole history of transactions in each block that make up Bitcoin's blockchain is irreversible. Tampering will get detected easily, as this system helps to establish an exact and transparent order of events, whereas anyone can transparently see all transactions.

If this was too technical of a description, let me make the analogy to spreadsheets. Imagine one giant spreadsheet, where you're not allowed to alter rows on the spreadsheet. This action will get verified and validated by a network of decentralized computers for correctness. If you would try to tamper with the spreadsheet by including (unethical) actions (that would benefit you), the network would collectively reject the addition of that row to the spreadsheet, as the spreadsheet and all the transactions can be viewed by everyone on the blockchain.

Because transactions are trackable and irreversible, and exist across a distributed, decentralized blockchain network, the platform can get used to create smart contracts. A smart contract is a contract with the terms of the agreement between buyer and seller being directly written into lines of code, which makes the contract self-executing. The code controls the execution.

If you want to understand a concept, you're better off when you apply first principles thinking. Oftentimes we get through life by copying what other people do or listening to what they tell us to do, which is reasoning by analogy. "First principles thinking is the practice of actively questioning every assumption you think you 'know' about a given problem and scenario, and then based on your own reasoning create new knowledge and solutions from scratch", says Elon Musk, and he sure knows a thing or two about that.

Blockchain-based non-fungible tokens:

Blockchain technology allows the generation of tokens with metadata of any type of information that the creator/author wishes to generate and include in the work or in the digital asset that he is creating. Among others, the identification of the author, the qualities or materials with which the file was created, the receiver or the identity of the buyer, are some of the data that can be included in the NFT tokens.

The NFT art and how to sell art with non-fungible NFT tokens based on Ethereum ETH and Blockchain technology

As he tokenization of artistic creations based on Blockchain technology allows the creation of a new market for transactional digital works with cryptographic assets, all based on Ethereum (ETH), one of the thousands of cryptocurrencies. Can you imagine all the technologies yet to be discovered in the other cryptocurrencies?

Digital art begins to be auctioned for hundreds of thousands of dollars

A trend that could make illustrations, videos and other digital works like GIFs and memes worth millions of dollars and all thanks to a certification of authenticity and ownership called Non-Fungible Tokens or NFT.

In March 2021, Christie's, the prestigious British auction house, announced that for the first time in history a work of digital art was auctioned for $69.7 million. This is unprecedented, making its author one of the three most valuable living painters in the world.

This technology raises the same speculation as the world of cryptocurrencies (Bitcoin, Ethereum, Cardano, Ripple, etc.) But very few have bothered to learn how the block system works and what makes this technology so powerful to identify, authenticate and record objects, identities, transactions, _etc._

I always think that delving into highly complex technology is a minimum requirement to safely invest in blockchain-based digital assets, and even more so, decide to create crypto-based projects or startups.

These cryptocurrencies are based on a system that records every transaction that happens – the blockchain. The blockchain spans several functions. One of which smart contracts.

Blockchain was designed to be unhackable. However, smart contracts' involvement has created some openings through which bad actors can sometimes enter and cause trouble.

Bitcoin and Ethereum, the two most popular cryptocurrencies, are supported on public blockchains, which have the higher defensive ability. Still, when it comes to smart contracts, the shorter, less complex codes involved means that more people can participate if you will call NFTs a form of using smart contracts for good.

Nick Szabo introduced the idea behind smart contracts. Following the original definition, a smart contract represents a set of promises, specified in digital form, including protocols within which the parties perform on these promises.

Smart contracts have been implemented on blockchains and are used mainly as a general-purpose computation that takes place on the blockchain (i.e. sets of actions on which parties agree to be executed). This enables decentralized computational logic, which extends Blockchain Technology's application to more than just cryptocurrencies.

Ethereum Blockchain

The introduction and adoption of smart contract interface standards have aided the development process of decentralized applications. This has facilitated a consistent application interaction and created, managed, and transferred tokens universally and uniformly.

ERC20 and ERC721 are just two of the most popular established token standards. The former is the initial token standard on Ethereum that provides basic functionality to transfer and manage fungible tokens, equivalent to crypto that functions as fiat.Do not get freaked out with ERC; it is an acronym that stands for ***Ethereum Request for comments***, illustrating the open-source model of getting community feedback from the beginning. Since ERC20 tokens are fungible, they are divisible in terms of value. The latter standard has been officially accepted only recently, and it has opened a new range of application opportunities.

Flow

Ethereum blockchain is not the only blockchain that has the capacity to host NFTs. As the market grows, there has been an increasing number of players offering blockchain technologies to NFTs.

Flow is one of such blockchains. The website list Flow is a fast, decentralized, and developer-friendly blockchain, designed as the foundation for a new generation of games, apps, and the digital assets that power them.

Binance Smart Chain

Binance is known to most people as a crypto trading platform; it is more than that. Not only does the platform have its coin, the BNB, it also has its blockchain – the Binance Smart chain. The Smart chain is optimized for fast load time.

NFTs are one of the critical building blocks of a new, blockchain-powered digital economy. Several projects are experimenting with NFTs for various use cases, such as gaming, digital identity, licensing, certificates, and fine art. What is more, they can even allow fractional ownership of high-value items.

Let us run over the details again:

NFTs or Nonfungible tokens represent a part of the blockchain where tokens are not fungible, that is, divisible, or one can be given in exchange for another. This makes NFTs ideal for the creation, sales, and distribution of unique digital assets.

Unlike fungible cryptos or fiat currencies, NFTs are limited by virtue of creation. The scarcity is essentially what drives the value. NFT has been used in the sales and distribution of artworks and even virtual real estate.

NFT is built on a blockchain – the Ethereum blockchain and it utilizes the ERC721 designation on the blockchain. In recent times, there have been new blockchains that have the capabilities to host NFTs; these include Flow and Binance Smart Chain.

NFT addresses the issue of ownership in the digital space. By purchasing an NFT, the blockchain records you as the one who is in possession of the token. It does not mean that the artwork cannot be used elsewhere;in fact, you will most likely see the artwork you own on the internet if it is popular enough. What matters is that you own it. That is what NFT is about.

Think of it as purchasing an album off Spotify, yes, you can listen to the album, but someone owns it. It is the same way when someone uses a digital copy of an NFT that is owned by someone else.

Today, there is increasing attention being paid to Nonfungible tokens and the potential it holds in revolutionizing the arts and systems of ownership. Nonfungible tokens (NFT) have become the digital assets that represent a wide range of unique tangible and intangible items, from collectible sports cards, trivia items to virtual real estate and even digital sneakers.

Anything can become an NFT; the photograph of your feet, a digital painting, a music album, a film, empty space in some virtual country. The potential for NFT is limitless, so how do you get started?

Select the dedicated site of your choice

There are a number of dedicated sites you can use to create your NFT. You can decide to use Rarible, Mintbase, or Cargo. One important quality in choosing a dedicated site is to know the blockchain the site functions on.

Is it the Ethereum blockchain, the Binance Smart Chain, Flow by Dapper Labs, Tron, EOS, Polkadot, Tezos, Cosmos, and WAX?We have gone into a bit of how the Ethereum and Flow blockchain works. Mintbase works with the Ethereum blockchain.

Cargo is synonymous with the Flow Blockchain. If you have a preference for some particular blockchain, you can always find the dedicated site that matches the blockchain of your choice.

Choose your NFT art

Once you have picked out a dedicated site of your choice, you should create an account and click on create a new item or create a new NFT as the case may be. If it is a music album, ensure you have it in mp3 format. If it is a picture, save it as a jpeg or png extension and upload it. The process is seamless and fast. Remember that anything can be an NFT.

Add your description and other details before your NFT goes live. Details to be added include the percentage of royalty you would choose to be paid if the NFT is sold at a later date. Ensure you go through the phases before clicking done.

Accept the charges

For every NFT minted and put out in the world, there is a charge that comes with it. On the Ethereum blockchain, it is referred to as the gas fee.

This is the amount charged for the maintenance of the blockchain, once you accept the charges, it is deducted from the crypto wallet linked to the account, and the NFT goes live, making it available for bidding and purchase.

The charges should be around $5. It can be much higher depending on the level of congestion within the blockchain at the moment in time.

Your first NFT is out for purchase. All that is left is to wait as the bidding process starts. No one knows how much Pebble has paid in gas fees; some can get lucky, some others not so lucky.

Blockchain protocols behind the NFTs

Currently, most of the NFTs are issued in the Ethereum blockchain. The token standards to create NFTs are compatible with other blockchains, as long as the blockchain protocol uses a Turing-complete programming language.

Blockchains such as Cardano, EOS and Tezos also support the creation of NFTs (at least in theory). However, it seems that the community prefers to continue to use the Ethereum blockchain, although the network is quite congested, generating very high transaction fees.

The explanation on why people prefer to continue using Ethereum instead of other blockchains is, in my opinion, due to network effects. The Ethereum network is where everyone is issuing NFTs, and for that same reason, people continue to use it. A network gets more valuable when more participants join it. The more participants a network has, the better the network's value and the capacity to conduct business in the network grows.

How Can One Sell And Buy Nfts On Ethereum?

Selling NFTs

Remember the three criteria that are key for producing artistic work: uniqueness, no tampering and notion of provenance. So if you wanted to create your own cryptoart and sell it, you'd have to fulfill these three criteria. But that's not enough. With that basic understanding in mind, you then create your artwork. Whether that's a simple .gif, photo, video, or music or similar is totally up to you. But that's not all. The important step is that you then want to tokenize your artwork.

Tokenizing

When you "tokenize" your art, you're basically linking the work you've created to a blockchain by creating a token that represents a good or an asset. (Meaning, the token by itself has no value. Your artwork will have some unique metadata attached to it with a unique link to your artwork that's hosted somewhere else.) This process will allow you to prove ownership and creates a permanent timestamp.

So your artwork, together with the token you create that includes a unique link with metadata, will then make up what's called Cryptoart. NFTs are simply pointing to assets, they are not the things themselves. Think about the famous image of the pipe with the French words "ceci n'est pas une pipe" (this is not a pipe). This also means, we're not at a point yet where physical art itself can become an NFT easily, as you can't 'link' to it to tokenize it.

For all of you wondering how to avoid that someone will claim ownership over your artwork, remember that it not only takes the artwork itself, but more importantly the token (unique metadata link that only exists once). So while anyone can copy your art work, no one will be able to copy and own your one-of-a-kind token but you.

A non-fungible token traces any official artwork back to the artist. All owners will get recorded on the blockchain.

Edged

Edged is an internet archive tool that permanently timestamps and stores web pages directly into the Bitcoin BSV blockchain. All etched pages are permanently stored, and the web content is available forever. It's independently provable by anyone who has access to the bitcoin blockchain.

Minting

NFTs are tokens that get 'minted' once they are created, using the ERC-721 Standard (more on that in a sec). Minting an NFT is how your digital art becomes a part of the Ethereum blockchain.

Since you hold and manage your funds directly on Ethereum you have to create a digital wallet first, and then add the crypto coin Ether (ETH) to your wallet.

(Digital) Wallet

There are many digital wallets available online, such as MetaMask, Coinbase Wallet, Rainbow, MeetDapper and others. I'm not promoting one or the other, or any, as a matter of fact. So if you're interested in learning more about that, do your research, please. Also, each of the digital wallet providers will tell you how you can add Ether into your wallet.

There are two types of commonly used wallets; 'cold wallets', as well as 'hot wallets'. Cold wallets are physical devices (think memory stick, external hard drive and things like that) that store your cryptocurrency inside of them. Hot wallets on the other hand are digital cryptocurrency wallets (think desktop or online). While hot wallets may be more popular of the two, you may still want to do your research on cold wallets as well. One of the advantages of a cold wallet is the fact that it's not exposed to attacks from cybercriminals. Hot wallets, because they are digital wallets, store security keys and codes on their online server, which could potentially get hacked. When you buy a cold wallet, you keep your codes and security keys on an actual, physical, little device (which bares the risk that you can lose it.). There are providers entering the market now that offer you sort of a hybrid. One example is CoolWallet S, where you store your cryptocurrency offline, but it's also accessible to you via their mobile app. Again, I'm not promoting this provider, I'm just giving you pointers for your research. Do your own security and cost comparison, please.

ERC-721 Standard

Speaking of security. ERC-721 is the standard used for safe NFT transfers introduces a standard for NFT. It's a free, open standard that describes how to build non-fungible - meaning unique - tokens on the Ethereum blockchain. The tokenId includes name, symbol, total supply, ownership, and other globally unique identifiers. Functions include safely transferring tokens from one account to another, providing data on the total supply of a token available on the blockchain and ownership of that token, showing the current token balance of an account, and others.

Chapter 4: Types

NFTs are being utilized as means of trading elite things online and they can possibly be utilized to check whatever would have esteem in demonstrating possession. Indeed, even tweets can be traded as NFTs. For instance, Twitter CEO Jack Dorsey for the first time ever, sold his own tweet in March 2021 for a huge number of dollars, changing the returns over to Bitcoin and giving them to good cause. Albeit advanced things can be exceptional, there is likewise esteem in things which might possess various duplicates yet hold an incentive for authorities, for example, sports exchanging cards.

Nonfungible tokens can be utilized to cause fake shortage of a computerized inventive job by causing just a single non-fungible token that work with an exceptional mark. NFTs of various artworks are hence like signed things. The remarkable character and responsibility for NFT is undeniable by means of the blockchain record. NFTs have metadata that is prepared through a cryptographic hash work, a calculation that figures a different kind, 40-digit arrangement of numbers and letters. NFTs are likewise used to create the opportunity of resource interoperability across different stages.

Advanced Art.

Advanced workmanship was part of the early use cases of non-fungible tokens, in cognizance of the capacity of blockchain innovation to guarantee the remarkable mark and responsibility for.

Games.

NFTs can likewise be utilized to address in-game resources which are constrained by the client instead of the game engineer. The main utilization of non-fungible tokens in gaming was executed by Tokenzone utilizing a brought together methodology. NFTs permit resources for be exchanged on outsider commercial centers without authorization from the game engineer. Computerized Assets At the point when we refer to Decentraland, individuals can purchase virtual land. Another model more recognizable to home is the ENS (Ether Name Service), and it utilizes NFT's for its. Ether spaces to assist with purchasing and trading.

Nonfungible tokens are critical for vetting for ID misrepresentation. Cases of things which may be made digital to address personality incorporate capabilities, clinical reports, and looks. Besides, computerized makers can transform their items into NFTs for patent rights thoughts. NFT's utilization to check character includes transforming actual sports tickets into *non-fungible tokens to* stay away from fakes.

Digital Assets

Think of Decentraland. Here, participants can buy virtual land. Another example that is closer to home is ENS (Ethereum Name Service), which uses NFTs for its .ETH domains to facilitate buying and selling.

Identity

NFTs are ideal for fighting identity theft. Examples of things that can be digitized to represent identity include academic qualifications, medical records and even our appearances.

Furthermore, digital artists can turn their work into NFTs for copyright purposes.

NFT's use to prove identity includes converting physical game tickets into non-fungible tokens to weed out counterfeits.

Collectibles

NFTs bring a new dawn to the collectible world. Consequently, conventional collectors are now onto digital assets.

Chapter 5: High value Nft

One of the key differences between cryptocurrencies and NFTs is that the supply of a cryptocurrency is fixed. The supply of an NFT can change depending on the creator's intention.

The economics behind supply and demand will dictate how much your token is worth. If there are a lot of tokens available, it will be more difficult for people to sell them for a high price because there are many other people trying to sell their tokens as well.

This concept is most important when thinking about digital collectibles (like CryptoKitties). When CryptoKitties were first released, there were very few kitties in circulation. Each kitty was worth a lot of money because there were very few kitties available.

Now that there are thousands of CryptoKitties in circulation, the price of each kitty has decreased because it's much easier for people to sell their kitties at a high price because there are many other people trying to sell their kitties as well. The same concept applies to any NFT.

If you want your token to be worth a lot of money, you should try and make it scarce so that there are fewer tokens available in circulation.

Why NFT'S are expensive?

Traditional digital assets have existed for many years now, but they haven't really changed much over the years. With NFTs, however, there is a possibility that they will change a lot in the coming years. They can change by becoming more secure, by getting more adoption from developers and gamers alike, and by getting more widespread support from exchanges and other organizations.

Because of this, NFTs could become far more valuable than traditional digital assets. This is because of their potential to create true ownership over in-game items and even other things such as land or even tangible goods such as cars or houses in the future.

Another reason why NFTs are so special is because they are truly open source for anyone who wants to use them in their games or on their platforms. Because of this, developers can create unique games and applications without worrying about copyright infringement or other legal issues that may arise when using NFTs with other technologies like blockchain technology or smart contracts. This is because everything is already built into the NFT protocol, and everything is open source.

However, there are still some challenges that developers will need to overcome if they want to make NFTs a reality for everyone. These challenges include the fact that NFTs can only function with blockchain technology or another similar technology. This means that most developers don't have the right technical knowledge or resources at their disposal in order to create NFTs for their games.

Chapter 6: NFT Market

How to buy and sell Nonfungible tokens

NFTs are exchanged in cryptographic forms of money, so you first need to purchase digital currency and hold it in a wallet. You at that point need to set up an account with an NFT commercial center, like Nifty Gateway, OpenSea or Rarible. Deals regularly appear as selloffs with a beginning NFT cost, so on the off chance that you enter a triumphant offer you will take responsibility for NFT. On the off chance that the worth thusly rises, you can set up your own bartering on a commercial center to sell it for a benefit. While purchasing a NFT doesn't move the copyright for the work, it gives essential use rights like posting a picture on the web.

Nonfungible tokens can be bought on an assortment of stages, and whichever you pick will rely upon what it is you have to purchase (for instance, on the off chance that you have to purchase baseball cards you're best making a beeline for a site like digitaltradingcards, however different commercial centers sell more summed up pieces). You'll require a wallet explicit to the stage you're purchasing on and you'll have to fill that wallet with cryptographic money. Nonfungible tokens can be bought on different online marketplaces such as Rarible, NFT Showroom, BakerySwap, VIV3, OpenSea and others.

If you're not an artwork creator but are more interested in buying NFTs, how would you go about that? You'd have to do some marketplace research first. Once more, I'm not here to promote any marketplaces. I'm just giving you some ideas on where you can start to look.

Opensea is currently the largest NFT marketplace, according to their website. A beginner-friendly mint and market platform is Rarible. If you're more into auctioning collectibles, you may find Niftygateway a good choice or Makersplace. And art lovers may tend to go with KnownOrigin or Superrare.

Who are the stakeholders of NFTs

1. Developers

The developer is the person or company that creates the game and owns the code. They are in charge of deploying the game to the blockchain, maintaining it, and adding new features to it.

The developer can be a centralized entity, such as a game studio or blockchain company. Or they can be a decentralized team, such as an open-source community of contributors. In most cases, NFTs will be launched by developers on top of an existing blockchain protocol (such as Ethereum). The developer then creates a smart contract to support their game. The rules of this smart contract determine how the NFTs are minted and transferred between players in the game. The developer also determines what happens when NFTs are destroyed or abandoned (more on this later).

2. Players

The player is any person who plays a game using NFTs and owns them at some point during gameplay. There are many different types of players in any given NFT-based game: first-time users who want to learn how to play; casual players who enjoy regular gameplay; and expert players who participate in high-stakes tournaments with prizes like cars or houses. A player may play just for fun, but they may also play for financial gain.

3. Collectors

The collector is any person who owns NFTs for investment purposes. The most common type of collector is an NFT investor, or someone who purchases NFTs in order to sell them at a higher price in the future. There are many other types of collectors as well, including speculators and NFT traders. Collectors are interested in any game that uses NFTs, regardless of how popular it is. Some collectors are highly selective about which games they support, while others collect as many different types of games as possible.

4. Traders

The trader is a player who specializes in buying and selling NFTs to make a profit. They can be players or collectors, but their primary goal is to buy low and sell high rather than to play the game itself. Most traders are active on secondary markets such as centralized exchanges or decentralized exchanges (DEXes). A DEX is an online market where buyers and sellers can trade with each other directly without the use of a middleman (like an exchange). There are several ways that traders make money from NFTs: they can sell them at higher prices than they paid; they can short sell them; or they can trade them on margin.

5. Speculators

The speculator is a player who buys NFTs in order to sell them at a higher price in the future. They may buy NFTs from other players or from the developer, depending on their strategy. For example, they may purchase an NFT at a discount during its presale period and then sell it for more once it becomes more popular. Or they may purchase an NFT that is highly sought after by collectors and hold onto it until it appreciates in value.

6. Investors

The investor is a player who purchases NFTs as part of a portfolio of assets (or with borrowed money). They expect to make a profit on their investment over time through price appreciation or dividends (more on this later). The most common type of investor is an asset manager, or someone who manages other people's money and uses investment strategies such as value investing, growth investing, or momentum investing. Investors can also be hedge funds, family offices, angel investors, venture capitalists, and others. They are interested in any game that uses NFTs regardless of how popular it is. However, most of them are more selective about which games they support than collectors are.

Risks associated with Purchase and sale on NFT

Like any new resource that is in the beginning phases of advancement and appropriation, NFTs convey some danger similar to far from mass acknowledgment. In the event that a financial backer picks to purchase a NFT and interest in exchanging them consequently slows down or even disappears, costs will fall and the purchaser could be left with huge misfortunes.

NFTs are not absolved from misrepresentation. NFTs professing to be crafted by notable specialists have been sold for a huge number of dollars however have been uncovered to be phony. Furthermore, similarly that digital forms of money can be taken, NFTs can possibly be dependent upon burglary relying upon how they are put away. Another danger to consider is that computerized content isn't altogether liberated from weakening in quality, record designs getting out of date, sites going disconnected briefly or even forever, or the deficiency of wallet passwords. For makers, printing NFTs to sell content doesn't ensure legitimate rights to responsibility for work, giving less assurance from burglary than they may anticipate. While NFTs and the commercial centers that sell them are decentralized, there can in any case be obstacles to acquiring section and openness for their work. A significant number of the stages are greeting just, similarly as craftsmanship exhibitions and other actual scenes select specialists to address. Since **NFTs can be** created dependent on essentially anything computerized, and that advanced things can be effectively duplicated, there's **the potential for** misuse. In particular, there's nothing preventing anybody from making *their own NFT* dependent on computerized things created by others. In one model announced by Decrypt on March 13, craftsman "Odd Undead" has discovered individuals taking advanced *works of art from* their tweets. The pictures were utilized to create NFTs and were sold on a NFT commercial center, deals that the craftsman has attempted to end. Bizarre Undead alludes to the training as "crazy and trivial copyright encroachment," one which just advantages the commercial centers and individuals taking the pictures, not simply the craftsmen. The training isn't simply restricted to fine arts. There have likewise been issues with individuals tokenizing tweets by others as NFTs and selling them. Once more, the training doesn't include the individual who composed the first tweet, who might eventually possess **the copyright for the** content. While it is totally conceivable for a craftsman or the maker of media to sue under existing brand name *and intellectual property* laws, *the idea of* how blockchain works can make it hard to discover who initially encroached *to make the NFT*. There's additionally *the issue of* which commercial center to trust in any case. Different blockchain administrations could each guarantee they have records that a particular NFT is interesting, *and that they are* the expert *for the work*. **This is what** might be compared to two closeout houses asserting they are the scene of offer for an extraordinary piece of craftsmanship.

Right now, it seems to be that there is a level of participation between significant commercial centers regarding the matter, however there has been no assurance things will remain as such later on. Include that it is therefore workable for individuals to set up their own commercial centers on blockchains, and it gets more diligent to police the non-fungible tokens as being set available for purchase. These are issues that should be tended to eventually, both in order to make sure of the occupation of specialists and to keep the deals of NFTs legitimate. For the occasion, these issues haven't blunted the craving for all around obeyed purchasers. For Nadya Ivanova, COO of L'Atelier BNP Paribas, a developing statistical surveying firm that teamed up with Nonfungible.com on a report on non-fungible tokens in February, the innovation's most noteworthy strength is additionally one of its significant shortcomings. Anybody on the web can make a NFT out of in real circumstances, anything, which implies there are a lot of "truly downright awful" out there, Ivanova reiterated in the meeting. It takes a prepared eye to remove what merits gathering or putting resources into. "That applies to the actual workmanship market too — it's normally a space for the educated. Same thing with NFT craftsmanship," Ivanova said. Also, despite the fact Ivanova views the NFT market as at last developing and proceeding with its course into the standard, she perceives a modest bunch of extra dangers and vulnerabilities new gatherers ought to consider about the maturing space.

The non-fungible token market experiences huge unpredictability, Ivanova said, to some degree on the grounds that there aren't any instruments set up yet to help individuals value resources. Throughout 2020, the estimation of probably the most famous kinds of NFTs spiked by around 2,000%, L'Atelier's report found. On the Top Shot, few features that at first traded for a couple dollars are currently worth many thousands. As regarding liquidity — how promptly a resource can be traded for money — NFTs are much more like baseball cards or art pieces than bitcoin or stocks, in cognizance of the circumstances, each merchant needs to discover a purchaser who will address a specific cost for a specific, unique thing. That can place authorities in a troublesome spot on the off chance that they, say, burned through $100,000 on a top-notch second the marketplaces start to tank, Ivanova said. Yet, illiquidity can likewise be something to be grateful for, since it keeps individuals from settling on careless choices, Andrew Steinwold, a crypto financial backer who began a NFT venture store in September 2019, told Insider. In the event that individuals don't have the alternative to freeze and offload their NFTs, the market could keep off from the sort of falling qualities that would start such a selloff in any case, he said.

NFT Marketplace

The NFT marketplace is any marketplace where NFTs are bought and sold. This can be a centralized exchange, a decentralized exchange, or a specialized trading platform for NFTs. The NFT marketplace can also be the game itself, if the game supports in-game trading of NFTs.

The most well-known marketplaces and minting platforms are **SuperRare, OpenSea, Rarible, Nifty Gateway**, but there are more. Be aware of fake websites. Like any other industry, when there's a lot of money flowing, scammers are trying to rip off people's money.

These marketplaces can be used both by creators and by art collectors to create the NFT, and buy or sell it.

It is also important to say that most of the marketplaces use Ether as a cryptocurrency, but sometimes other cryptocurrencies can also be accepted.

Nifty Gateway is the platform where Beeple famously sold his artwork. Nifty is an invitation-only platform for artists, **i.e.** to sell on Nifty you will need to be invited.

Currently, OpenSea is probably the biggest NFT marketplace where you can list NFTs minted on many other platforms.

NFT Economics: The Factors that Influence Demand

The demand for an NFT is determined by many different factors, including scarcity, provenance, condition, desirability, utility, liquidity, and speculation. Some of these factors are unique to non-fungible tokens (NFTs), while others are shared with traditional fungible tokens (such as bitcoin and ether). In this section we'll explore each factor in more detail. We'll start with some basic economic concepts that are relevant to both types of tokens before we dive into how they apply to non-fungible tokens specifically.

NFTs can be used to represent anything, including physical objects. For example, an individual could create a digital token that represents a share of their house. This token could then be used as collateral for a loan or as proof of ownership for their house.

When an individual wants to create a NFT, they need to be aware of how it will affect the supply of the item being represented by the token. For example, if you create a digital token that represents 1/100th of your house, there are now 99 tokens representing 1/100th of your house in circulation (instead of 100).

Another way to think about this is through scarcity. If there are only 100 tokens representing 1/100th of your house, each token has a higher chance at receiving some value because there are fewer tokens available and they are more scarce. It's much easier for people to sell their tokens to other people because they are not competing with other individuals who have a similar share of your house.

Does NFTs have a fixed supply like BTC?

NFTs can have a fixed supply, a limited supply, or an unlimited supply. A token that has a fixed supply is similar to a cryptocurrency with a fixed supply. In the case of NFTs, each NFT is assigned a unique identifier (ERC-721) and can be tracked as it moves from one owner to another.

In the case of CryptoKitties, each CryptoKitty is uniquely identified by its own 256-bit genome that consists of these genes:

- Attribute: This gene defines the cat's appearance and gives it its special abilities.
- This gene defines the cat's appearance and gives it its special abilities. Genotype: This gene determines the cat's genotype. It consists of 256 bits that determine the DNA sequence for this specific CryptoKitty.
- Cutype: This gene contains information about how many times this specific CryptoKitty has been bred or sired by other cats in the network. For example, if a CryptoKitty has a "1" in this gene, it means that it has sired or been sired once.
- Cowner: This gene identifies the owner of the CryptoKitty. The owner can be the person who bought the CryptoKitty, a third party, or the CryptoKitty itself.

The owners of a CryptoKitty can also be changed through the use of a smart contract. In this case, the CryptoKitty's owner is simply the person who owns the private key to the Ethereum address that contains this particular CryptoKitty. This makes it possible for third parties to own CryptoKitties and use them as part of their business models.

To summarize, each CryptoKitty has a unique 256-bit genome and an owner who can change over time. The current owner is determined by the private key of an Ethereum address that contains this specific CryptoKitty. In order to change ownership, you must first change ownership in a smart contract and then sign off on it with your private key (in case of a multi-signature smart contract). This makes it possible for someone to "purchase" a unique and rare 256-bit genome in order to breed new cats with special abilities (for example, see KittyVerse).

Unlike other cryptocurrencies, there is no limit on how many NFTs can be created. Instead, NFTs are created in two ways: through "creation" or through "breeding."

Creation: NFTs can be created in the same way that cryptocurrencies are created. This is done by the creation of a new smart contract that contains all of the attributes of a new CryptoKitty.

Breeding: In order to create new NFTs, they must first be bred with other NFTs in order to produce offspring with specific and unique characteristics. For example, a KittyVerse developer might want to create a CryptoKitty with special abilities (for example, unique appearance or certain attributes). In order to do this, they would need to breed this CryptoKitty with another CryptoKitty that has similar or complementary attributes (such as appearance).

The breeding process is somewhat similar to traditional genetic engineering techniques where an organism's DNA is manipulated in order to produce offspring with certain characteristics. However, instead of using genes from existing organisms, you use blockchain-based smart contracts as your DNA blueprint. The process of breeding NFTs is called "breeding" and the act of breeding NFTs is called "siring."

To summarize, NFTs can be created in two ways: through "creation" or through "breeding." In the case of creation, a new smart contract is created that contains all of the attributes of a new CryptoKitty. In the case of breeding, you use blockchain-based smart contracts as your DNA blueprint to produce offspring with specific and unique characteristics.

Investing in NFTs

Can/should NFTs be seen as an investment?

NFTs represent a unique asset, and as such, they may have value. The value of an asset such as art is sometimes abstract, but the value usually corresponds to whatever people believe it's worth and what people are willing to pay for it.

Digital art was until now, hard to track and hard to prove which of the copies was the original. Digital art is very easy to copy when compared to a physical painting, for example. But NFTs allow now artists to tokenize a file and say, "this one is the original". Digital art can, for the first time, be considered unique, ownable and tradeable.

In 2016, the Number 17A by Jackson Pollock was sold for $200 Million. Why? Well, the answer is simple: because the purchaser believes it's worth $200 Million.

When talking about physical art represented by an NFT, the collector needs to understand what are his rights when purchasing the NFT. Although the market is very new, there are usually a few options to digitize physical work and represent it on an NFT:

- Option one: the artists create a physical artwork and digitize it to create the NFT (through photography or other techniques) and keep both the physical art and the NFT. Both the physical item and the NFT are considered unique and ownable. The physical art can either be sold separately or be sold together with the NFT.

- Option two: digitize the artwork and destroy the physical artwork. It may make sense to destroy the physical artwork in order to make the NFT totally unique. The destruction of the physical artwork can be recorded and shared with the owner of the NFT. A Banksy was bought for $95,000 by Injective Protocol, a blockchain company, and it was burned after being digitized into an NFT. A physical artwork can eventually be seen only as a means or a tool to create a digital NFT, and thus, it may make sense to destroy it or consider it only a study or mold for the final NFT, which leads us to option three.
- Option three: treat the physical artwork as just a tool for the tokenization process. Don't sell the physical artwork but only the NFT, which is considered the final version of the artwork.

In some cases, when an NFT is created from a physical artwork, the NFT ends up being worth even more than the physical version, which is an interesting phenomenon.

Regarding the value of an NFT, it is all related to the perceived value of the artist, the artwork and the supply and demand. Before buying an NFT, make sure you understand if that NFT is a unique NSF or if it is part of a limited edition of x number of NFTs.

To understand market trends and the value of a certain NFT, there are different marketplaces like OpenSea where it is possible to **check price trends** and a lot of useful information. Other platforms like **Nonfungible** and **Dappradar** also offer some analytics on NFTs.

Cryptopunks 90 days price history based on OpenSea marketplace.

Market Growth and Sales Mechanism

While NFTs have been around for some time – pretty much as long as the Ether cryptocurrency – some recent purchases have made it a headline technology. In March, a digital image created by the artist Beeple was sold for US$69 million dollars with an NFT attached to certify its ownership. In the same month, Twitter Founder Jack Dorsey put his first tweet on the market for $2.5 million. Going back three and a half years, the first real NFT bubble started with CryptoKitties, an app that sold "ownership" of virtual kittens for sometimes upwards of US$100,000.

We don't normally editorialise much in this column, but this month is going to be a little different, and I expect we might offend some blockchain adherents. While NFTs might not be a scam, precisely, they are at least scam-adjacent, driven largely by speculators looking for "the greater fool", in Wall Street parlance. They are a trade in completely imaginary assets – selling the concept of ownership without actually necessarily selling ownership of anything.

Chapter 7: How to pick NFT to trade for a 100x profit

So what does it mean to own an NFT? What does "ownership" in this context actually mean – for example, what does it mean to have an NFT representing a tweet or a CryptoKitty or a digital artwork? If TechLife's Editor would let me, I would probably put a shrug emoji right here (I have my limits, Nathan -Ed).

NFTs are legally and technically toothless, and can be likened to those services that, for $50, claim that they will name a star after you. It's not a scam, exactly – it's just kind of meaningless. It's a note in an online ledger without any legal or technical force in itself.

When you purchase an NFT on a digital asset it does not imply or legally mean that you've acquired ownership of the copyrights to that asset, unless the NFT comes with an enforceable contract specifying that it does. But in that context the contract itself is the only part that's relevant – the NFT itself is, again, meaningless.

Nor does it prevent anyone from copying the work through technical means. The person who paid $69 million for a JPG cannot stop anyone from making a digital or physical copy of the work, except through traditional copyright law enforcement (assuming they now own the copyrights, which, again, is not certain without a legal contract).

An NFT is simply an entry in an online ledger, in itself having no real-world value. Anyone can create such tokens at will and for no cost. It only has the value we assign to it – again, the subjective theory of value reigns supreme here. This is why these NFTs usually get associated with things that might seem valuable, even when there is no actual linkage between the NFT and the object in question other than the NFT creator's say so. Indeed, we're already seeing many scams where people are selling NFTs of things they don't own. One could create an NFT and say "this token certifies ownership of the Taj Mahal" and there's no-one to stop you.

Future Potential of NFTs

The future of non-fungible tokens is uncertain. The current value is not sustainable and the market is overpriced, but this doesn't mean that there won't be a recovery. There are a lot of people who believe in the future of NFTs and crypto art, so there could be a rebound in the near future. We can only wait and see what happens to the market in the next few months or years.

The idea of a digital asset which has ownership, which can be exchanged and traded, is not new. Crypto-collectibles are essentially digital assets that are designed to be unique, and only one instance of each token can exist. This has created a marketplace for collectibles where users can purchase and trade these tokens.

The future of crypto-collectibles is very bright, with more and more users entering the market. Although there are some key challenges that need to be overcome before they can be considered mainstream.

The future of NFTs will heavily depend on the progress of the Ethereum network and wider blockchain technology.

It's safe to assume that as blockchain technology continues to grow, NFTs will follow – whether it's on the Ethereum blockchain, another public network, or a private network.

In this section, we will discuss the future potential of NFTs and how it will change the world.

Physical Goods Utility:

Physical goods utility is the idea that you can use an item to derive value from it. This is why many physical goods have a resale value.

For example, if you own a digital asset of your house, you can potentially use it as collateral for a loan. As long as the physical asset exists, the digital asset has value.

It's important to note that there are not any digital assets that currently offer this utility, however this is one of the main reasons why crypto-collectibles have gained so much popularity.

Non-Fungible Crypto-Collectibles are Proof of Ownership:

Crypto-collectibles are designed to be unique tokens which mean that they cannot be duplicated or forged. This creates a very unique digital asset which can be used as proof of ownership for certain physical goods. For example, if you own a CryptoKitty that is modeled after your pet cat, then there will only ever be one instance of this token in existence. You could use this token as proof of ownership for your pet cat, however there is no reason why you could not use it as proof of ownership for other physical goods.

In the future, we could see this type of utility being used for art, gold, real estate and many other physical goods. The idea that you can store your ownership of a physical good on the blockchain is a very exciting concept.

Think of it as digital inheritance. When you die, your digital assets are transferred to the rightful owners, and it's also a way to prove that you are the owner of an item.

The NFT Approach to Crowdfunding

The following video describes the NFT Approach to Crowdfunding, which is a new way for companies to raise capital. Since 2015, NFTs have been available on the Ethereum network. However, they still remain relatively unknown with game developers and their wider audience. This means that many developers may not have the tools or resources to create an NFT. This is one of the reasons that the NFT approach to crowdfunding was developed. This approach makes it possible for NFTs to be designed, hosted, and distributed on any platform (including mobile devices and web browsers). In addition, game developers can also build their own crowdfunding campaign using the "NFT-Crowdfund" standard. It provides developers with the tools and resources they need to create their own NFT. This allows them to create their own ERC-721 token, an NFT that can be used as a crowdfunding campaign.

NFT use cases in gaming

Here is how you can potentially build your own NFT-Crowdfund:
1) Create your own colored token for crowdfunding on a platform

(Ethereum Wallet, Metamask, etc.) or via a command line interface (console).

2) Use NFT-Crowdfund protocol for creating and distributing the NFT.

3) Use ERC 721 to describe your game items.

4) Use ERC – 684 for creating pre-order items with a discount. These will not be fungible after the Crowdfund ends. Unsold pre-order items are burned.

5) List your rare item(s) on a marketplace for selling post-crowdfunding using NFT registry, or create your own marketplace. Rename your NFT if needed to reflect the marketplace name. All pre-order items must be re-categorized to match your new marketplace category.

1) Create your own colored token for crowdfunding on a platform (Ethereum Wallet, Metamask, etc.) or via command line interface (console).

2) Use NFT-Crowdfund protocol for creating and distributing the NFT.

3) Use ERC 721 to describe your game items.

Protecting Digital Written Content:

The problem with written content on the internet is that it can be copied and shared with ease. However, with a NFT, this becomes a lot more difficult.

If you own a digital asset that represents your written content, then you can use it as proof of ownership. For example, if you own the digital asset of a blog post or article that you have written, then you can prove that it is yours and there is only one instance of it in existence.

The same principle applies to artwork and music. As long as the token represents ownership of the artwork or music file, then there will only ever be one instance of this token in existence.

Artwork or Music:

In order for artwork to be truly unique, the artist must design it specifically for the piece of art itself. This means that every single aspect must be designed by the artist themselves which means they will have complete control over how many instances exist on the blockchain. They will also have complete control over how they are used in the future (such as selling them on a marketplace). As long as an artist has designed their artwork for a specific piece of art and each piece is uniquely designed for each other, then there will only ever be one instance in existence on the blockchain. This means that you can prove ownership of the artwork without the risk of someone copying it.

The same principle applies to music. If an artist creates a specific piece of music and records it, then they can also prove ownership over that specific piece of music. The key difference between art and music is that in order for a piece of art to be unique, the artist must design it specifically for that piece of art. Whereas with music, it's more about recording the specific sound at a specific time in history. This means that if you own a token which represents your digital content, then you can use it as proof of ownership for any physical goods which derive value from this content.

Trading NFTs:

Crypto-collectibles are not only designed to be unique tokens which represent ownership, but they are also designed to be collectible items. This means that people will collect them because they want to own a large number of them and build up their collection. For example, people will buy CryptoKitties in order to build up their collection and add value to their collection by breeding them with other CryptoKitties or trading them on an exchange for ETH or other cryptocurrencies.

This is why many people think that crypto-collectibles will become a mainstream market in the future. As more and more users enter the market, it will create a huge demand for these tokens which could lead to an increase in their value.

In the future, we could see a shift away from buying NFTs for their utility value, and instead users will buy them as collectibles. This is similar to the way that people collect trading cards or rare coins. However, there are still many challenges that need to be overcome before this can happen.

Tackling the issue of digital counterfeit goods:

NFTs have the potential to create a digital library of sorts. You can store your music, art, books and collectibles in a digital library where no one can counterfeit them. As long as you own the digital asset, no one can take it away from you. This is one of the many ways in which NFTs are trying to address the issue of counterfeit goods.

For example, let's say you own a rare copy of Game of Thrones and want to sell it to someone. With the help of NFTs, you can store all the details about your digital asset in a secure blockchain and sell it to someone else.

In addition, you can also verify the authenticity of your digital asset by storing it in a digital library where other people can see that you are the owner of that particular digital asset. This is something which cannot be done with physical goods.

Tackling the issue of data ownership:

Another potential use case for NFTs is tackling the issue of data ownership. Right now, there are many centralized companies which own and store our data like Facebook, Google *etc*. And they don't give us access to our own data even if we want to get rid of them as our service providers. For example, if I am using Facebook or Google services, I don't have any rights over my personal data that these companies collect from me and use for their own benefit (to target ads). So, they are collecting my personal information like my location history, browsing history etc and selling it to third parties without my consent or knowledge (which is totally illegal).

But, NFTs can help us solve this problem. We can create our own digital assets like a website, blog or any other digital asset and store it in a decentralized platform. Then, we can sell these digital assets to other people. Once the transaction is done, no one can take away your data from you. So, if you are using Facebook or Google services, you don't have to give them access to your personal data (and you don't have to pay them for it). Instead, you can use their services and get paid for it by selling your digital assets to them.

This is the potential of NFTs that we haven't seen yet. As more and more platforms are going to be built on top of Ethereum, we will see more applications of NFTs in the future.

Authenticating Land Ownership:

Land ownership is one of the biggest issues in the world today. You can easily find out if someone owns a land or not by looking at their public records, but it's not easy to prove that you own a land.

For example, let's say you own a land in Canada and want to sell it to someone else. In order to do that, you will have to go through a lot of paperwork and follow a very long process. Not only that, you will also have to pay heavy taxes for selling your land. And after all this, there is no guarantee that the buyer will not steal your land from you later on. This is because most of the time people can forge their documents and make fake IDs.

So, how can NFTs help solve this problem?

NFTs have the potential to create digital identities for land owners which can be verified by anyone using blockchain technology. In addition, we can also store information about our lands in an immutable ledger which cannot be forged or tampered with. So, if you are trying to sell your land in Canada then anyone who is interested in buying it can verify your ownership of that particular piece of land just by checking out the public records.

In addition, you can also prove that you own a land by showing your digital identity to the person who is interested in buying it. And this will be much easier than showing them your physical documents and proving that you own a land.

Chapter 8: A list of NFT projects I'm going to invest in 2021

NFTs—an emerging technology that uses crypto platforms to authenticate ownership of digital files. During the last crypto boom, the region—home to some of the cheapest power in the U.S.—was beset with a new energy-hungry home industry: basements and sheds loaded with racks of computers churning through advanced mathematical calculations in order to "mine" valuable crypto coins like Bitcoin and Ethereum. But even small crypto mines can overload local grids, making them a problem for energy companies. Far larger cryptocurrency mines have been set up from Texas to Iran to China's Inner Mongolia.

That may surprise artists and other NFT fans who are far removed from the technology's environmental toll. "You don't see your money is going to a miner who's going to pay for fossil-fuel-based energy with it," says Alex de Vries, a financial economist.

Some in the crypto world are working on solutions. Ethereum's developers promise to launch a less energy-intensive approach by 2022. But cryptocurrencies are popular in part because they're decentralized, which attracts people who distrust governments. That means there's no single leader who could force a change.

NFT Topmost Projects

NFT-focused projects and products have improved in tandem with the rapid development of the NFT subspace. The top four NFT projects are listed below.

1. ***OpenSea:*** This is the best place to buy and sell NFT collectible and art. The marketplace accepts a variety of virtual currencies, including ETH. Virtual pets, ENS, and land plots are among the items listed. Notably, the marketplace accepts a variety of virtual currencies, including DAI and ETH.

2. ***Async.Art:*** Async is another marketplace for non-fungible tokens where you can purchase, sell, and create non-fungible tokens. It also allows customers to purchase and change pieces of "layers" of an artwork. The platform has several programming features that allow artists to easily define the appearance and actions of their work. In reality, it enables customers to customize parts or "layers" of a piece of artwork that they bought.

3. ***CryptoKitties***: This project deserves to be at the top of the list of NFT projects because it brought the NFT game to the forefront. Even though we've already covered this project, it still needs to be included in our top NFT projects list since it launched the entire NFT industry.

4. ***The Ethereum Name Service (ENS):*** This is a design for a domain name service that was released in mid-2017. ETH domain names are non-fungible tokens (NFTs) that use Ethereum's ERC-721 designs and can be traded in the NFT market. The .ETH domain names are non-fungible tokens (NFTs) that follow Ethereum's ERC-721 specifications and can be traded on NFT exchanges.

5. ***Decentraland:*** is a top NFT project that focuses on a distributed virtual environment. Participants can purchase virtual land here. In addition, each "inhabitant" has a unique digital passport that identifies them.

What is driving the current rise in NFTs?

The recent explosion of blockchain-based collectibles, particularly on the Ethereum blockchain, has created a new class of asset that can be owned by anyone in the world and which has been dubbed Crypto Collectibles.

While this sounds exciting to many people, there is still a lot of confusion about what exactly a crypto collectible is and how it differs from other crypto assets such as cryptocurrencies.

Is there a market bubble for NFTs?

Going back to the basics of a bubble, there is clearly an extreme spike in the value of non-fungible tokens. But, how long will this bubble last? This is a question that only time can answer. It is possible that NFTs are in a bubble and that the bubble will pop, but we won't know for sure until the market adjusts to a new price.

1. Speculation

The crypto market is full of speculators and people who believe that they can predict the future. These people have been buying NFTs in hopes that the value will continue to rise. This type of behavior isn't necessarily a bad thing, but it can create a bit of volatility. When the market fluctuates, some people get hurt and others make money. The goal is to make money, but many people aren't able to predict how high or low the price will go.

2. Media Attention

Many of the top NFTs are being used in games and virtual worlds. There are some crypto art projects that are making it big in the media and social circles. When something gets this much attention, it is easy for speculators to jump on board and buy NFTs at a higher price. When there is more demand for NFTs, the price will increase.

3. Limited Supply

There are a limited number of NFTs that are being created each year for each project. The amount of tokens that are available at any given time is being reduced because of the projects that are creating new tokens. Some people believe that this reduction in supply will lead to a higher price, but it isn't necessarily true. A higher price will only occur if there is more demand for the tokens.

4. The rise in popularity of decentralized games and virtual worlds

The popularity of decentralized games and virtual worlds is on the rise. There are many projects that are creating new games and virtual worlds that will utilize NFTs. Some of these projects have been successful, while others have failed. When a project fails, it could mean that the value of the NFTs associated with that project will decrease.

Chapter 9: How to easily create an NFT and sell it

Get A Digital Wallet

Commonly Used Ethereum Wallets Include Metamask, Ledger Nano X And Coinbase Wallet; Think Of These As Crypto Checking Accounts.

Load Your Wallet

You'll Need To Convert Your Real-World Cash Into Cryptocurrency In Order To Pay The Necessary Transaction Fees To Create Your Nft.

Connect Your Wallet With An Nft Platform

Popular Platforms Include Nifty Gateway, Opensea And Superrare; Some Are Invitation-Only.

Upload And Sign Your Art

Nfts Can Be Images, Gifs, Audio Files Or 3-D Models. Sign Your Nft To Assert That It's Authentically Yours.

Mint Your Nft

Most Nft Platforms Charge A Fee To Upload New Files; The Cost Can Range From $40 To $200 Depending On The Conversion Rate.

Set Your Terms

Use a standard contract, or customize your options—you can choose to be paid every time your work is resold, for instance.

Congratulations, you have minted your first NFT. Now, list your artwork for sale and wait for the offers to roll in. Good luck

What takes place in a NFT transaction

1. The producer, or token issuer, is responsible for setting the rules of a game or experience and defining what happens when a user performs an action. The producer can also set the price that users pay to play.

2. The player/user buys access to the game with a non-fungible token (NFT). They may use ETH or other NFTs as well.

3. The player/user interacts with the game using their NFT, which triggers actions and/or events on the blockchain, like transferring ownership of a virtual asset or being awarded a prize. If they win something valuable, they can sell it on an exchange for ETH or other NFTs.

4. Other players may want to buy access to the same game with their own NFTs, but they can't unless they buy one from someone who already owns it. In order to acquire a NFT, you must trade another one for it or purchase it directly from the issuer (the developer). If you choose to trade your NFT for another one on an exchange, you'll be subject to market forces just like any other tradable asset—including volatility and transaction fees!

5. This loop continues until the game or experience ends.

Conclusion

Thank you for making it through to the end of this book. NFTs are based on a similar principle. It's an immutable record stored in an online ledger. They mostly started with Ethereum, the blockchain platform used for the Ether cryptocurrency, but have since spread to other platforms. They were intended to be used somewhat like a certificate of ownership, particularly for digital assets.

Non-Fungibility is the property of a good or a commodity whose individual units are considered unique. A Non-Fungible Token (NFT) is a crypto token that has this property.

In other words, if we think of it in terms of the real world, it is like having a share in an asset like gold or silver. The shares are not fungible and are all unique because they represent the asset.

Anybody can create an NFT, but there are some important steps, and you need to understand the technologies behind it, its features and constraints.

I will guide you through the steps and good practices to create an NFT so that you can be confident that you also do the right steps when you create your first NFT.

You don't need any coding skills to create an NFT, but you need to follow some steps, have a wallet, buy some crypto for gas and sign the transaction.

The Tokenisation of nonfungible assets has created endless possibilities for blockchain asset digitization. Blockchain offers the collectible market much more security and digital scarcity, especially to ensure assets' authenticity and eliminate counterfeiting. NFTs are popular in the gaming ecosystem, but besides gaming, NFTs can be used to digitize anything considered to have value.

Many people still miss this, but it is really important to break down the NFT creation into two sections. First, there is the blockchain which handles the minting and bookkeeping of the NFT. Blockchain is great to make sure that the metadata of the NFT is immutable and secure by replicating it across thousands of computers/nodes across the world. However, blockchains cannot handle storing large amounts of data because it becomes extremely expensive to replicate large amounts of data across those thousands of nodes. This is where the second section comes into place: storing the NFT data. The majority of the NFTs data needs to be stored off-chain, and we need to maintain this data too.

Good luck

CPSIA information can be obtained
at www.ICGtesting.com
Printed in the USA
BVHW050333080521
606757BV00010B/1301